BRADLEY PARK

Pride of Tomahawk, Wisconsin

ROBIN L. COMEAU

Copyright © 2021 Robin L. Comeau

Printed in the United States of America

Bradley Park: The Pride of Tomahawk, Wisconsin/ Comeau 1st Edition

ISBN: 979-84854130-2-6

1. Title.
2. Bradley Park/ Parks and Recreation.
3. History- United States- Wisconsin- Tomahawk.
4. History.
5. Historic Record.
6. History-Pictures-Images.

No part of this book may be reproduced or transmitted in any form by any means, electronic or mechanical, including photocopying, recording, or by any information storage and retrieval system without permission in writing by the author.

NFB
NFB Publishing/Amelia Press
119 Dorchester Road
Buffalo, New York 14213

For more information visit Nfbpublishing.com

For all who enjoy the pines.

Slanting North —

A hunger lingers in all of us to live in the natural world. We need to watch eagles take flight from high pines, to hear the wild sounds of cranes from secluded marshes, to smell pungent balsam needles in the dense woodland, to breathe clean sharp air that flares the nostrils. Our affinity for the natural world is why we fill our homes with plants, keep dogs and cats as members of our family, and escape the urban world to rural landscapes as often as possible. It is an innate force within us that draws us upnorth. While the Northwoods can be pointed to on a map, it is also a state of mind.

- John Bates

Bradley Park
Pride of Tomahawk, Wisconsin

Robin L. Comeau

Bradley Park

Pride of Tomahawk, Wisconsin

A pictorial essay including park history

Images sourced from the author's private collection, the Tomahawk Area Historical Society and the Tomahawk Leader Newspaper Archives

The Tomahawk and *The Tomahawk Leader* newspaper clippings were obtained from the Wisconsin State Historical Society newspaper microfilm collection

By Robin L. Comeau

Cover photo – The Hog's Back | Bradley Park

Postcard from the Tomahawk Area Historical Society collection

Introduction

Anyone familiar with Tomahawk, knows that Bradley Park, or the Hogs Back, as some choose to lovingly reference it, needs no formal introduction. The park trails, the pines and the water are woven into the lives of those who live in the area, those who visit for the first time, and those who return time and time again. There is just something about that *up north* feeling you get, walking beneath the 250+ year old pines and hiking to the 'point' that remain with a park visitor, whether the first or the 101st time through.

The park land consists of about 110 acres immediately adjourning the city on the west. The city of Tomahawk acquired a portion of the area that is now known as Bradley Park in 1910 for a cost of $10,000 from the interests of the city's founder, William H. Bradley. Based on information reported in local newspapers, the land was first acquired in 1910 through a land contract; $2000 payable per year with 4% interest, with the deed and payment of $10,000 conveyed June 24, 1920.

The early residents of Tomahawk knew Bradley Park as the Hog's Back, a name that refers to the glacially formed ridge that runs the length of the park. The ridge was likely formed during the last ice age by a river that flowed under the glacier. It is likely the same ridge that splits Somo Lake and supports several gravel pits in the city. The steep slopes of the Hogs Back and the large boggy areas surrounding it, made the area unattractive for industrial and residential development, but its beautiful timber and sparkling waters made it the favorite location for Tomahawk's citizens and visitors to relax and recreate. Even before being purchased by the city, the area was heavily used for year round recreational purposes; swimming, boating, camping, tobogganing, skiing and hiking.

Camping was popular and encouraged at the time of acquisition and the park was thrown open to tourists in the summer of 1922. Visitors arrived in droves with their campers and set up camp at one of two sites - in the midst of the timber or near Mirror Lake.

Facilities were planned and developed to accommodate the interest of both visitors and area residents. A swimming beach was developed which included changing facilities and docks. Private individuals leased water frontage and built boat houses offering boat and canoe rentals. The steep hills, soon became known to locals as *Deadman's* and *Suicide*, *Army* and *Navy*. A ski-jump, bob-sled and toboggan run complete with elevated ramps and a warming shelter were constructed for winter recreation. A two story wooden bandstand was erected and soon became a popular destination for celebrations and meetings as well as for the Chautauqua held in each summer. Works Project Administration (WPA), part of Roosevelt's New Deal in 1935, added a stone and log shelter as well as a separate restroom building, including supplying running water and electricity. Footbridges were built in the 1940s along with kitchen accommodations and stone barbeques.

Use of the park probably reached its peak between the 1930s and 1950s, but as America's recreational trends and travel patterns changed, traditional uses of the park also changed. As interest in the park declined at that time, so did the maintenance of the facilities. As vandalism increased, facilities deteriorated and had to be removed. Years of heavy, unrestricted use of the park by automobiles and camping vehicles compacted the soil and placed the health of the centuries old pines in danger. Steps to preserve the trees were taken and vehicles were restricted to roadways and parking lots. In 1976 the Park Board voted to prohibit overnight camping, with the same vote occurring the next year due to a pine bark beetle infestation; then in 1978 the board voted to prohibit overnight camping indefinitely.

Today, the park is as popular as ever, frequently used for hiking, biking and prior to the COVID-19 pandemic, class reunions, weddings and meetings. It remains a relaxing and popular destination for photo buffs, hikers, bikers, boaters, fishermen, snowmobilers, and ATV enthusiasts. Bradley Park is really Tomahawk's best known secret.

Take a walk with me as we stroll through the park's history in print and pictures, and embrace that *up north* feeling once again.

2018

Photos Through the Years

Launch parade at the point – early 1900s

Launch Parade

Log Rolling Contest with Bradley's Boat Train in back

Both images - Bradley's Boat Train

Bradley's Boat Train docked for the day

Boat House Bay

Bradley's Boat Train

Employees for Bradley's Boat Train 1893

The 'Nyack' made trips up the Wisconsin River with Mr. Bradley's house guests.
It had sleepers, a dining room and kitchen.

George Leville, Delia L'Abbe's brother, was the boat train pilot.

Both images - Boat house bay in Bradley Park

Both images – Private boat house offering boat rentals

Boathouse by Bradley Park

View of foot bridges from drive through Bradley Park

Early 1900s

Boathouses in the slough (Boat House Bay) near the Marinette Depot

Grandstand

Old Settler's Association gathering in Bradley Park early 1900s

1915 Chautauqua held in Bradley Park

Both images - Camp Grounds – Bradley Park

Camp grounds – Bradley Park

Tenting grounds in Bradley Park during 1915 Chautauqua

Bradley Park

View in Bradley Park

Celebration in Bradley Park

Bradley Park

Community House built by the WPA in the 1930s

Stone and log shelters built in the 1930s as part of the WPA projects.

Shelter House in Bradley Park

Mirror Lake in Bradley Park

Cabin by Mirror Lake

Foot bridge to the point

Roadway through Bradley Park

Foot bridge to Prospect Point 1913

1936

1935 Entrance to the Park

Prospect Point

Prospect Park Lake

Foot bridge to Prospect Point

Foot Bridge to Prospect Point

Boulevard drive to Bradley Park

Roadway through Bradley Park

Drive way through Bradley Park

Road way through Bradley Park

Mirror Lake Bradley Park

Mirror Lake in Bradley Park

Bradley Park

2019

Path to Mirror Lake Bradley Park

Looking across to the point (Prospect Point) – legend has it that an Indian Maiden was killed there by her lover; often referenced as 'Squaw Point'.

Swimming beach on Prospect Point Bradley Park

Both images - Mirror Lake Bradley Park

View of two footbridges – Bradley Park

Hogs Back July 3, 1909 - Modern Woodsmen Picnic Grounds

The Hog's Back

Both images - Toboggan Run in Bradley Park

Both images - Toboggan run in Bradley Park

Annual Tournament Here Next Sunday

The fourth annual tournament of the Tomahawk Ski Club will be held next Sunday afternoon, beginning at two o'clock on "Suicide Hill" in Bradley Park. Entries have been received for the three classes from the best riders in this vicinity and a keen afternoon of competition is looked for.

In addition to the open events to which all riders are eligible, there will be exhibition jumps by Clarence Biriling, of Ironwood, Mich., who has performed on the local slide on previous occasions.

The club will sell tags on Saturday and Sunday to assist in defraying expenses. There is no admission fee to the park.

Ski Jump in Bradley Park   January 1932

Over 50 area skiers took part in the first annual Ski Jumping Contest which took place on January 19, 1928 in Bradley Park.

WARRANTY DEED [transcribed by author from original deed]

No. 89737

This indenture, made this **24th day of June**, in the year of our Lord, **one thousand nine hundred and twenty**, between Bradley Company, a corporation duly organized and existing under the laws of Wisconsin and located at Tomahawk, State of Wisconsin, of the first part, and City of Tomahawk, a municipal corporation, party of the second part.

Witnesseth that the said party of the first part, for and in consideration of the sum of Ten Thousand ($10,000) Dollars, the receipt where of is hereby confessed and acknowledged, has given, granted, bargained, sold, remised, released, aliened, conveyed and confirmed and by these presents doth give, grant , bargain, sell, release, align, convey and confirm, unto the said party of the second part, its successors and assigns forever, the following described real estate, situated in the County of Lincoln, and State of Wisconsin, to – wit:

All that portion of the following descriptions which are not now overflowed by a head of water of 48" on the roll of the dam of the Tomahawk Land & Boom Company situated in Section Ten (10), Township Thirty-Four (34) North of Range Six (6) East, intending to cover by this description what is commonly known as the Hogsback Park, to-wit: All of Government Lot Three (3) of Section Four (4), Township Thirty-Four (34) North of Range Six (6) East. All of Lots 1,2,19 and 20 of Block 20; Lots 1,2,19,20 and 21 of Block 22; all of Block 24, and Lot 1 of Block 23, Thielman's Second Addition to the City of Tomahawk.

All that part of Government Lot Nine (9), Section Thirty-Three (33), Township Thirty-Five (35) North of Range Six (6) East, lying south of a line parallel to the north line of said Government Lot Nine (9), and 100 feet distant south from the same, measured at angles to it. All of the south one-half of the Southwest quarter of the Southeast quarter (SW1/4-

SE1/4), and all that part of the southeast quarter of the Southeast quarter (SE1/4-SE1/4) of Section Thirty-Three (33), Township Thirty-Five (35) North of Range Six (6) East, lying south and west of the right of way of the M.T. & W. R.R., and the C.M. & St. P R.R., also all that part of the Northeast quarter of the northeast quarter (NE1/4-NE1/4) of Section Four (4), Township Thirty-Four (34) North of Range Six (6) East, lying west of the right of way of the C.M. & St. P R.R., excepting as follows: Beginning at the southwest corner of said northeast quarter of the northeast quarter (NE1/4-NE1/4) and running thence northerly along the section line seventy-two (72') feet, more or less, to the center of the road called Putnam Street in the R.C. Thielman Addition; thence westerly along center of said road to the center line of Fourth Street in said addition; thence south at right angles to the north line of Government Lot 2; thence easterly along the north line of Government Lot 2, to the place of beginning. Also excepting and reserving therefrom the right always to cause to be overflowed all such portions thereof as may now or hereafter be overflowed by the waters of the Wisconsin River by means of the construction, operations and maintenance of a dam of any height desired in said river on Section Ten (10), Township Thirty-Four (34), North of Range Six (6) East.

This deed is made upon and subject to the express condition that the same, and the whole thereof shall be used solely for public purposes, and that said City of Tomahawk shall at all times use, keep and maintain the same, and the whole thereof, as a public park, and upon and subject to the express condition that if the said premises of any part thereof, shall be used for any other purpose, to the City of Tomahawk shall cease to use, keep or maintain the same, and the whole thereof as a public park, then the said premises and the title, interest and state granted and conveyed shall thereupon ipso-facto revert to the first party, its successors or assigns, without re-entry or declaration of forfeiture.

"Park purposes" (wherever the term is used in this instrument) shall be construed to include the use of said premises, or any part or parts thereof, by said City or by any person or persons, having the permission of said City, for Chautauqua, baseball, tennis, golf, playground, bathing and bath house purposes, boat house purposes as hereinafter more particularly specified, and such other purposes as shall be conducive to the amusement and recreation for the residents of and visitors to said City of Tomahawk, and be in the nature public, but shall not include the use of said lands or any part thereof, on the waters of the Wisconsin river or any subaqueous lands, either by said City or by any persons or persons with its permission for any other purposes that "park purposes" as defined in this paragraph, nor the use of any of the enumerated purposes when a charge is made for such use, or for gaining admission to any event, contest, amusement, or entertainment held or conducted on said premises, except when the premises are used for Chautauqua, baseball, or for boat house purposes, and within the meaning of this instrument the said premises shall also be deemed as used, kept or maintained for "park purposes" or as a "public park" when the same are not used or maintained for any apparent purposes whatever, or for any purpose inconsistent with the uses or purposes as included within the meaning of "park purposes".

"Boat house purposes" (wherever the term is used herein) shall be construed to include the use of said premises or any part thereof, for the erection and maintenance of any municipal boat house or boat houses and the use of such boat house or boat houses by any person or persons upon such terms, conditions and the payment of rent as said City shall prescribe, and shall further include the use of said premises for the erection and maintenance thereon of boat houses by such individuals or corporations as have the authority or permission of said City, upon such terms, conditions, and payment of rent as the City shall prescribe, or its duly authorized officers shall demand, except that no permission or authority shall be given or lease granted to any individual or corporation by said City, at any time, for the use of said premises, or any part thereof, for the erection or maintenance of a boat house thereon for a longer term than one year.

And it is further understood that the grant of permission by said City to Foster Brothers, revocable at will, to construct and maintain a sidetrack running east and west along the north side of Putnam Street in R. C. Thielmans's Addition to said City, from Tomahawk Avenue on the east to Fifth Street in said Addition to the west, and also over and across a strip of land on the south side of above premises, shall not be deemed or construed to be a violation of any of the provisions of this instrument.

This instrument is made pursuant to the terms and provisions of a certain land contract made by and between said Bradley Company of said City, dated April 27, 1910, also another certain land contract between said parties, dated July 9, 1918.

Together with all and singular, the hereditaments and appurtenances thereunto belonging or in anywise appertaining; all the estate, right, title, interest, claim or demand whatsoever, of the said party of the first part, either in law or equity, wither in possession or expectancy of, in and to the above bargained premusrs and their hereditaments and appurtenances.

To Have and To Hold the said premises as above described, with the hereditaments and appurtenances, unto the said party of the second part, and to its successors and assigns forever.

And the said grantor, for itself and its successors doth hereby covenant, grant, bargain and agree, to and with the said party of the second part, its successors and assigns, that at the time of ensealing and delivery of these presents the said party of the first part is well seized of the premises above described, as of a good, sure, and perfect, and absolute and indefeasible estate of inheritance in the law, in fee simple, and that the same are free and clear from all encumbrances whatever, and doth further covenant that the above bargained premises, in the quiet and peaceable possession of the said party of the second part, its successors and assigns, against all and every person or persons lawfully claiming the whole or any part thereof, it and they shall will forever warrant and defend.

In Witness Whereof, the party of the first part hath caused these presents to be signed by R. B. Tweedy, its President, its corporate seal to be hereto affixed, and these presents to be countersigned by E. C. McNaughton, its Secretary, the day and year first above written.

Signed, Sealed and Delivered in Presence of
Alice Doan.
Josephine Lando. 1-$20.00
Revenue Stamp
Cancelled and attached.

Bradley Company Organized Jan. 10, 1888, Wisconsin

BRADLEY COMPANY.
By R. B. Tweedy, President.
Countersigned:
E. C. McNaughton, Secretary.

State of Wisconsin,
County of Lincoln, } ss.

Personally came before me this 27th day of Sept. A. D. 1920, the foregoing named R. B. Tweedy, President, and E. C. McNaughton, Secretary, of the Bradley Company, to me known to be such officers, and to be the persons who executed the foregoing instrument, and they acknowledged the execution of such instrument as the act and deed of said corporation.

Received for record 18th day of November, A. D. 1920, at 8:01 A. M. o'clock.

[signature] Register.

Alice Doan,
Notary Public, Lincoln County, Wis.

Alice Doan,
Notary Public Lincoln County, Wis.
My commission expires Sept. 13, 1925.

In The News

WANT THE "HOG'S BACK"

Many of Our Citizens Think City Should Own It.

FINEST NATURAL PARK IN NORTH

Must Buy It This Summer or Pine Will Be Cut.

The "Hog's Back" just west of this city, is now commanding the serious attention of many of our citizens, as it is understood that the Alexander Stewart Lumber Company of Wausau, is now making arrangements to strip this beautiful natural park of its stately pines during the coming winter. In conversation with a representative of the above company a few weeks ago we were informed that as that company has very little standing timber in this vicinity, it has decided to close up its logging operations next winter and that the "Hog's Back" will be it's first camping grounds. But if public sentiment counts for anything—and it surely does—the "Hog's Back" will not fall a victim of the woodman's ax, because our citizens are too progressive, too enterprising, too public spirited to allow this beautiful spot to be robbed of its beauty, and we believe our city fathers will see to it that the "Hog's Back" will become the property of the city of Tomahawk.

During the last few years it has been suggested many times that the city should make an effort to purchase the "Hog's Back", but as long as the timber has been left standing, no move has been made in that direction, and it would seem that the time is now up to either "wake up" to the beauty of the place and its value to our city or remain in a doubtful mood and allow it to be destroyed.

March 25, 1905

WORK STARTED ON DRIVEWAY

Crew of Men and Teams Grading and Removing Obstructions on the Hog's Back.

Work was started Monday on the Hog's Back driveway. A crew of men and teams is grading and removing stumps, brush and stone. A bridge is also being built across the inlet alongside the foot bridge just south of the Marinette depot.

The amount of work done on the driveway will depend on the expense. If the making of the driveway is found to be not too costly, it will probably be completed this year. Enough work, however, will be done to make a fine walk around Tomahawk's beauty spot.

May 29, 1908

Work on the Hog's Back driveway is finished and the thoroughfare is now open for traffic.

June 5, 1908

TO PRESERVE DRIVEWAY

Improvement Association Takes Steps to Continue Good Work Done on Hog's Back.

Steps will be taken at once to further improve the Hog's Back driveway, so that the work already done will be preserved and not lost because of a lack of attention. At a meeting of the Improvement association Tuesday evening J. H. Butcher, J. L. Wakefield and H. J. Taylor were chosen as a committee to ascertain the nature of the work to be done and the probable cost. This committee will report at a meeting to be held next Monday evening.

Another improvement to be made on the Hog's Back is the driving of a well to supply water to picknickers and other visitors to Tomahawk's beauty spot. This good work is to be done by the Woman's Literary club, the money to meet the expense having been donated by the club members.

June 19, 1908

The committee having in charge the placing of a well and pump at a convenient point on the Hog's Back reported that this had been done, and a supply of first-class water found. This well will be a gratifying convenience to picknickers and other visitors, and the thanks of all is due to the Woman's Literary club, which furnished the funds for this important project.

June 26, 1908

A committee consisting of the president with H. J. Taylor and A. E. Sutliff, appointed to inspect the Hog's Back drive and report what steps are necessary in the immediate future to perfect and preserve it in the best condition, reported that from $100 to $200 could be spent on the driveway to good advantage, so as to place it in a condition that would continually improve and perpetuate the work already done. This drive extends practically from the Milwaukee railway park, about one and one-half miles around the Hog's Back and coming out at South Tomahawk. This drive was laid out according to the plans of Mrs. A. E. McCrea, the celebrated landscape architect, and is much the most romantic pleasure drive existing anywhere, at least in the Wisconsin valley. It is hoped the funds necessary to further improve the roadbed according to the plans of the committee will be rapidly forthcoming.

June 19, 1908

OLD SETTLERS TO GATHER

Residents of Tomahawk for Eighteen Years or More Invited to a Picnic Sept. 17.

The old settlers of Tomahawk will have a picnic on the Hog's Back next Thursday afternoon. Every old settler in Tomahawk who has lived here since the early days is asked by the committee to come with their families and their lunch baskets and talk over old days and have a good time.

It is the idea of those originating the picnic that if enough attend, an old settler's association will be formed similar to those of other communities where they hold annual gatherings and have a big time generally. There are a number of families that have been here more than eighteen years and many of them want to get together at least once a year "just for old time's sake."

September 11, 1908

OLD SETTLERS ORGANIZE

Seventy-five Early-Comers Gather at Picnic and Decide on Annual Gatherings.

The first old settlers' picnic and re-union, held on the Hog's Back Thursday afternoon, was a greater success than anticipated. About seventy-five were present with lunch baskets and enjoyed a good time, recounting experiences of the early days in Tomahawk.

An organization was effected to be known as the Old Settler's Association of Tomahawk. Officers elected were:

President—Andrew Oelhafen.
Secretary—Floyd A. Clark.
Treasurer—C. E. Macomber.

The officers together with three ladies to be selected by the president, will form a committee to make arrangements for the next re-union and picnic to be held next fall. The first Wednesday in September was selected as the date for the annual meetings. The membership is open to everyone who has been a resident of Tomahawk eighteen years or more.

September 18, 1908

TO IMPROVE PARK DRIVEWAY

New Thoroughfare on the Hog's Back Will Be Graveled and Made More Permanent.

Further improvements, tending to make it more permanent, are to be made to the driveway on the Hog's Back. The work will be started Monday at the point where the road begins near the Marinette depot. The road will be widened at every turn and the soft, sandy stretches of road will get a top dressing of gravel and cinders. The work will be done by the Improvement association. A committee from the association met last evening and decided on the work. There is now a fund of $115 and the committee is planning to raise more money for the work. The improvements to be made will depend upon the amount of money raised. The driveway has been much appreciated by Tomahawk people and visitors to the city who have been over the route during the summer.

October 9, 1908

FOREST FIRES START AGAIN

Many Points in Northern Wisconsin and Michigan Report Renewed Invasion by Flames.

Several brush fires were reported as burning Tuesday and Wednesday. One fire was about four miles west on the Spirit Falls road and nearly all of the farmers in that neighborhood were called upon to fight the fire. Another brush fire was burning Wednesday afternoon northeast from the tannery. No serious damage is reported.

Thursday the air was smoke-laden in every direction and the glow from fires both west and north of town could be seen in the sky last evening.

Daily papers today brings reports of fresh fires at different points in northern Wisconsin and upper Michigan. An engine, hose cart and firemen were sent last night from Milwaukee to Foster City, in the upper peninsula of Michigan, as that village was seriously threatened by forest fires.

A fire in the grass at the edge of the Hog's Back grove near Tomahawk avenue caused an alarm Tuesday afternoon. The fire started near the railway track and spread through a young growth of Norway pine, damaging many of the trees. Men with shovels and several ploughed furrows prevented the fire from running far.

October 16, 1908

Fire starts near Hogs Back (last paragraph)

TO INCREASE DRIVEWAY FUND

Big Dance to Be Given Next Friday to Raise Money for Hog's Back Improvement.

To raise additional funds for the Hog's Back driveway a big dance will be given at the opera house next Friday evening, Oct. 23, under the management of the Tomahawk Improvement association. Arrangements for the dance are not yet completed, but the price of admission will probably be $1 a couple.

The improvements making to the driveway on the Hog's Back are of a nature that will be much appreciated by people who go over the road in future years. When the drive was made this summer, only enough was done to make the road passable. Now, the sharp turns in the driveway, and the approaches to the bridges across the sloughs are being widened and railings will be put on the bridges. Wherever the road is sandy, a surface of gravel and cinders will be put on. On the ridge, the drive is rough and stony. It is planned to take out the worst rocks and fill the holes with gravel.

As much work will be done as possible with the funds the Improvement Association has available. Through the generosity of several of the warehouse owners the fund will be increased $100 or more. Several of these men have agreed to donate to the fund all or part of their share of the money raised to help them move their warehouses.

Three men and a team have been used on the work of improving the driveway this week. H. J. Taylor is supervising the job.

October 16, 1908

DRIVEWAY FUND IS GROWING

BIG DANCE TONIGHT TO RAISE MONEY FOR HOG'S BACK

Warehouse Owners Contribute $300 to Aid In Good Work on Tomahawk Beauty Spot.

Many who haven't danced in years are figuring on going to the dance tonight at the opera house, and, of course, all of the young folks had their minds made up to go as soon as they heard of it. The tickets are $1.00 the couple and the Tomahawk orchestra will play the music. Everyone is invited to come to the dance and enjoy themselves.

The proceeds will go to swell the fund for improving the driveway on the Hog's Back. The Improvement Association is back of the affair and everyone is helping the association in its good work.

The dance committees are:
Reception—Dr. and Mrs. J. D. Cutter, Mr. and Mrs. R. A. Pride, Mr. and Mrs. W. D. Lambert.
Floor—Dr. G. R. Baker, P. H. Paul, H. J. Wakefield, H. H. Kuehling.
Arrangements—A. E. Sutliff, H. J. Taylor, Andrew Oelhafen.

Three hundred and six dollars has been added to the driveway improvement fund through one source alone. A number of the warehouse owners have generously agreed to donate to the fund their share of the money raised to aid them in removing their warehouses to the new site from the grounds since made into the railway park. The improvements making to the driveway are considered excellent so far as they have gone. About $100 has been expended. This generous giving by the warehouse owners, with what is raised by tonight's dance, will aid greatly the good work. The Hog's Back driveway is something which will be appreciated for many years to come.

October 23, 1908

1930

MORE WORK ON HOG'S BACK

IMPROVEMENT ASSOCIATION TO SPEND $200 OR $300

Bandstand, Benches and Surfacing of Driveway Is Planned—Association Elects Officers.

Between $200 and $300 will be expended this spring by the Tomahawk Improvement association on the Hog's Back. About $75 will be used in furthering work on the driveway which was made through the grove last year. Several sandy spots in the road need a top dressing of cinders. Work on the driveway was started Wednesday under the supervision of H. J. Taylor.

Other improvements to be made on the Hog's Back will include a bandstand, 24 feet in diameter, and a number of benches to be placed in convenient spots. It is probable too that something will be done at the Point to prevent further washing away of the sand and gravel. Two of the Norway pines on the Point have been nearly undermined by the waves.

Members of the Improvement association gathered at the library room of the city hall Monday evening and discussed plans for the coming season, especially the work to be done on the Hog's Back, which it is hoped to have completed in time for the coming Woodman picnic.

April 23, 1909

CITY MAY ACQUIRE HOG'S BACK

Proposition for Lease of Beautiful Park and Its Ultimate Purchase to Be Heard by Council.

A proposition for the city of Tomahawk to acquire a lease of the beautiful natural park known as the Hog's Back and to assure an opportunity to buy the park when the city can afford it, is expected to be up for discussion at the May meeting of the city council next Tuesday evening. It is said that a liberal offer has been made to the city by the Bradley company, the present owner of the property.

Public sentiment appears to favor the ownership of the park by the city, but it now rests with the council whether or not the deal can be made at present.

The much discussed dog question will also probably be laid before the council by Mayor M. C. Hyman.

April 30, 1909

First published report of Bradley Company's offer of park land to city.

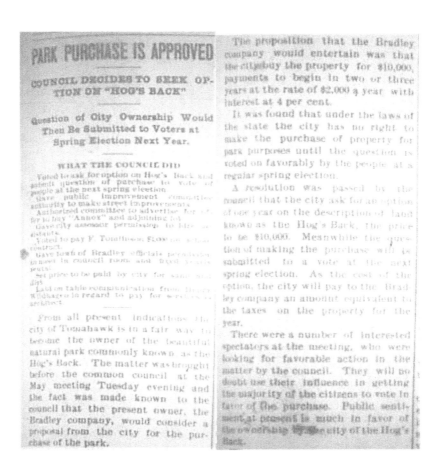

May 7, 1909 – To vote on matter next spring

Bradley Company offer stipulated that the city would buy the property for $10,000, payments to begin in two or three years at the rate of $2000 a year with interest at 4%. The deed filed in 1920 includes information that land contracts between the city and the Bradley Company dated April 27, 1910 and July 9, 1918 were made prior to the deed filing.

BOAT CLUB HOUSE PROPOSED

Owners of Craft Organize and May Erect Building to Replace Many Small Structures.

A new organization, to be known as the Tomahawk Boat club, was effected Tuesday evening at a meeting of boat owners held at the Mitchell hotel. Officers and directors elected are:

President—F. P. Werner.
Vice-president—H. J. Taylor.
Secretary—Henry Hickey.
Treasurer—J. L. Extrom.
Directors—William Drever, John W. Oelhafen, W. T. Bradley, Glenn Foss, C. H. Grundy.

Plans are making for a club boathouse to be built somewhere along the shores of "Boathouse Bay," where each member can have a separate stall or compartment for his boats. It is also planned to have one part of the boathouse built as a sort of rendezvous for the members. The plan is to have as many boat owners as possible join the club and if possible keep their boats in the proposed new building. Then the more unsightly boathouses that line the bay will be removed.

It was decided that the officers devise ways and means for the construction of the boathouse and that the secretary canvass for new members.

Another meeting will be held next Wednesday evening at the Mitchell hotel.

May 7, 1909

HOG'S BACK IMPROVEMENTS

Bandstand to Be Completed Next Week—New Footpath Made and Driveway Improved.

Improvements thus far planned for the Hog's Back are near completion and the park will be ready in plenty of time for the Woodman picnic July 3.

The latest work is a new footpath starting at the first bridge of the driveway and skirting the shores to the mouth of the lagoon, where bridges have been built to the little islands. The path is a short cut from the boat houses to the grove on the point of the Hog's Back. Lumber for the footbridges was donated by John Oelhafen and the Tomahawk Lumber company.

The new bandstand will be completed by next week. Railings have been put on the bridges of the driveway and the driveway itself has had much more work expended upon it. H. J. Taylor has been in charge of the work this spring.

Quite a sum of money has been expended on the Hog's Back improvements, which include the driveway, bridges, footpath, bandstand, boat landings and pump. Now it is up to Tomahawk people to enjoy these conveniences while they are able and not let them be misused.

May 14, 1909

Bandstand, foot path, additional foot bridges

How to Drive on the Hog's Back

To avoid confusion and possible collisions when driving over the Hog's Back driveway, members of the Improvement association have deemed it necessary to suggest that the start over the driveway be made at the end near the Marinette depot. There are a number of places in the driveway where rigs can safely pass one another, but the road is narrow in some stretches, especially on the slopes, making it awkward for rigs to pass. It is hoped that this suggestion will be observed on Sundays and on the day of the Woodman picnic when there will be much travel over the road.

May 21, 1909

OLD SETTLERS' PICNIC SEPT. 1

DATE SET FOR SECOND GATHERING OF FIRST-COMERS

President Oelhafen Names Arrangement Committee for Annual Meeting to Talk Over Old Times.

The second annual picnic and reunion of the Old Settlers' Association of Tomahawk will be held Wednesday, Sept. 1. President Andrew Oelhafen of the association has appointed a committee of arrangements for the picnic as follows: Mrs. O. K. Welty, Mrs. Richard Dawson, Mrs. Joseph A. Ball, and the officers of the association.

The first picnic was held on the Hog's Back last Sept. 17 and was attended by about seventy-five of the early residents of the city. Everyone who has lived in Tomahawk around eighteen years is eligible to membership. President Oelhafen states that there are a number of young people who were born in Tomahawk in the early days who are eligible to membership and who have not yet joined.

May 21, 1909

WILL CLEAN THE HOG'S BACK

Raking Bee, with Lunch and Plenty of Exercise, June 5 in Preparation for Woodman Picnic.

A "raking bee" will be held Saturday, June 5, on the Hog's Back. Everybody in Tomahawk who can get away is invited to attend the "bee." Bring your rakes along and a lunch and stay all day. It will do people good to "get back to nature," to enjoy a regular picnic and help in getting the grove "spick and span" for the approaching Woodman picnic.

May 28, 1909

RAKING "BEE" TOMORROW

Children Will Picnic and Help Clean the Hog's Back for Woodman Picnic on July 3.

If the weather is clear tomorrow, a big turnout of school children and their elders is expected at the raking "bee" on the Hog's Back. The children will assemble at 9 o'clock in the morning at the Whittier school. From there, headed by the band, they will march to the Hog's Back with rakes and lunch baskets and put in the day cleaning the grounds and picnicking. Lemonade will be served in any quantity to the workers.

President Andrew Oelhafen of the Improvement association has appointed a committee to superintend the work consisting of Supt. L. W. Brooks, Rev. J. B. Scheyer, Rev. I. H. Lewis, Rev. F. W. Heberlein, Rev. L. C. Kirst and Mssrs. Eli Hebert, W. D. Lambert, G. M. Sneldon, R. G. Lee and August Zastrow. Everyone else is invited to attend.

June 4, 1909

PICNIC PROGRAM IS READY

PLANS FOR GREAT WOODMAN EVENT PROGRESS RAPIDLY

Arrangements Practically Completed for Biggest Gathering in History of Tomahawk.

With the exception of a few details, the program for the big Woodman picnic on July 3 has been completed. Practically all arrangements for the great event are also made. Indications now point to the largest gathering in the history of Tomahawk. From several nearby cities come reports of Woodman delegations who will attend with bands and drill teams. Nearly every camp in the Northeastern Picnic association has reported the election of delegates. Maids of honor have also been elected by many camps.

Entertainment for the visitors will not be lacking during their stay in Tomahawk. Something will be doing from early until late.

Tomahawk will put on a gala attire for the event, too. Wisconsin avenue, from Railway to Fourth street, will be resplendent in Woodman banners and emblems, American flags, bunting in the national colors, and electric lights. Added to this, will be decorations on business houses and residences.

June 25, 1909

Modern Woodsmen event to be held in Bradley Park (pt. 1)

Miss Grace Whitson Is Queen

Miss Grace Whitson was elected Woodman queen in the contest which began May 31. The vote at the close of the contest last night was:

Miss Grace Whitson	880
Mrs. Georgia Gray	160
Mrs. H. H. Kuehling	30
Miss Dora LeMay	30
Miss Lillian Flynn	20
Miss Alva Fitzgerald	10
Miss Pauline Roper	10
Mrs. W. T. Bradley	10
Mrs. A. M. Pride	10

Events on the program and their order as decided upon are:

Horse races on Wisconsin avenue up to 11 o'clock.

Exhibition and prize contest drills by Woodman teams on Wisconsin avenue.

Parade at 12 o'clock to picnic grounds at Bradley park.

Launch parade headed by steamer Angus Buie with Tomahawk band aboard.

Dinner at picnic grounds.

Addresses.

Launch race on Wisconsin river off Bradley park.

Launch rides for visitors.

Band contest for $150 prize.

Dancing in new pavilion all afternoon.

Dance at opera house in evening.

June 25, 1909

Modern Woodsmen event to be held in Bradley Park (pt. 2)

Launch Parade a Feature

One of the important features of the picnic will be the parade of beautifully decorated launches. A committee consisting of C. H. Wallis, William Drever and C. H. Grundy has been appointed to make the necessary arrangements for this part of the program. Prizes of $10, $5 and $3 will be given for the best decorated boat. It is important that every launch owner in the city should turn out. It has been arranged that the fleet, headed by the Angus Bule, with the Tomahawk brass band on board, shall come into the bay immediately after the arrival of the parade from the city, which is expected to be at noon. The boats will then come to anchor for the picnic dinner. Following the speaking, which will come immediately after dinner, will come the launch races, for which arrangements are now being made. Those desiring to enter the races should report at once to the above committee.

June 25, 1909

Modern Woodsmen event to be held in Bradley Park to include Launch Parade of boats (pt. 3)

Launch Parade

Plans for Horse Races

E. C. Thielman, M. C. Hyman and Andrew Oelhafen have been appointed a committee on horse races. Those having horses to enter should see the committee at once. The purses have not been decided upon at this time.

A number of lunch boxes have been ordered for the Ladies' Aid societies and other organizations. They will be on sale at D. C. Jones' store July 1. Societies wishing these boxes may see a sample at the Jones store and they should be spoken for at once.

Woodman decorations may be secured of J. L. Wakefield, chairman of the decoration committee.

A bureau of information for Woodmen will be opened on the morning of picnic day, probably at the city hall. Here Woodmen may secure information in regard to the city and about places to lodge and eat. As the hotels will fill up early, it is desired that any one having rooms to rent of the visitors notify the arrangements committee at once, so that a list of the available sleeping accommodations may be prepared and the visitors assigned without delay or inconvenience.

June 25, 1909

Modern Woodsmen event to be held in Bradley Park
to include horse races on Wisconsin Avenue (final pt.)

THEY RACED HORSES DOWN WISCONSIN AVENUE IN TOMAHAWK ON JULY 4, 1908. SPECTATORS IN WINDOWS HAD CHOICE SEATS.

They raced horses down Wisconsin Avenue on July 4, 1908

OFFER PARK INTEREST TO CITY

TWO BRADLEY STOCKHOLDERS READY TO MAKE GIFT

Mrs. Marie H. Kelly and W. T. Bradley Send Proposal to Common Council.

Tomahawk may become the owner of the now famous Bradley park, known until recently as the Hog's Back, without cost to the city.

At the special meeting of the common council Tuesday night, communications were received from Mrs. Marie H. Kelly and W. T. Bradley, stockholders in the Bradley company, offering to donate to the city their interest in the park. The only provisions attached to the offer are that the other owners donate their interest, that the park be named the W. H. Bradley park and that it be properly cared for.

Mayor M. C. Hyman appointed a committee to confer with the other stockholders of the Bradley company and see what they are willing to do. Appointed on the committee were Andrew Oelhafen, R. C. Thielman and J. W. Froehlich.

July 2, 1909: Hog's Back offered at no cost

While this offer was reported, it did not stand, as the city first leased (under land contract) and then bought the property for $10,000, finalized on June 24, 1920. It is of interest to note, that this was the first time that *Bradley Park* was mentioned as a replacement name for Hog's Back. Both were used interchangeably in these early years since.

WOODMAN PICNIC A SUCCESS

TOMAHAWK ENTERTAINS 1,500 TO 2,000 VISITORS

Ideal Weather Brings Out the City's Largest Gathering to Enjoy a Splendid Program.

The Woodman picnic was a success. This is the consenus of opinion of both home people and visitors.

Conservative estimates place the number of Woodmen and other visitors in Tomahawk last Saturday at 1,500. At least 1,000 visitors were brought by trains on the Milwaukee road. All trains over the M., T. & W. railway were crowded. Undoubtedly the number of visitors passed the 1,500 mark. Between 3,000 and 4,000 people were on the streets and at Bradley park during the day and without doubt the gathering was the largest in the history of Tomahawk.

Fair, cool weather made the day ideal for the occasion. Visitors were in a gala mood. The townspeople entered into the true spirit of hospitality. If anybody failed to enjoy the day, it was no fault of the arrangements or the weather.

Bradley park was praised unstintedly by the visitors and the fame of Tomahawk's beauty spot surely will be spread still further.

Merrill sent a delegation of 500 or 600 to the picnic—not all Woodmen, of course, but a jolly good crowd who entered into the spirit of the occasion and showed Tomahawk a real neighborly feeling.

July 9, 1909

PRAISES BRADLEY PARK

Neenah Man Thinks It Most Beautiful Place He Ever Saw.

"I don't know whether your people appreciate it or not, but I think you have one of the most beautiful natural parks I ever saw anywhere," said J. R. Bloom of Neenah, speaking of Bradley park. Mr. Bloom arrived Wednesday to spend several days on business in connection with his duties as state factory inspector. While here he was also given a launch ride on the rivers and was much pleased with the scenery. The Somo river trip especially pleased him, the stream being "just as pretty as it is crooked." Mr. Bloom is publisher of The Neenah Daily News.

July 16, 1909

OLD SETTLERS PICNIC SEPT. 25

SECOND ANNUAL GATHERING OF FIRST COMERS

Invitation Extended This Year to Everyone to Attend Basket Dinner and Program at Bradley Park.

Tomahawk's old settlers will gather for their second annual picnic on Saturday, Sept. 25, at Bradley park. This year the gathering will not be confined to old settlers alone, an invitation being extended to everyone to attend.

Plans for the picnic are maturing rapidly. At a meeting of the arrangements committee Monday, the plans were gotten under way. It was decided that a basket picnic be held, the Old Settlers association to serve hot coffee. Picknickers will furnish their own eatables and plates, cups, knives, forks and spoons.

While not definitely decided, it is expected that a program of speeches and music will be arranged for the afternoon. Officers of the association will also be elected.

The arrangement committee Monday selected an entertainment committee as follows: Mr. and Mrs. C. E. Macomber, chairmen; Mr. and Mrs. A. J. Olson, Mr. and Mrs. A. M. Pride, Mr. and Mrs. W. D. Lambert, Mrs. Mary E. Headstream, Miss Emogene Wentworth, Floyd A. Clark.

The members of the arrangement committee are Mmes. O. K. Welty, Richard Dawson and Joseph A. Ball. This committee will also serve as a dinner committee.

The Old Settlers' association was organized last year at the first annual picnic with a membership of about thirty. Officers chosen are: President, Andrew Oelhafen; secretary, Floyd A. Clark; treasurer, C. E. Macomber. It is expected this year to greatly increase the membership.

September 10, 1909

OLD SETTLERS MEET TOMORROW

Annual Picnic to Be Held at Bradley Park—Dinner, Speeches and Songs the Program.

The second annual picnic of the Old Settlers association will be held tomorrow (Saturday) at Bradley park. After a picnic dinner at noon, the afternoon will be devoted to speeches, patriotic and old-time songs and other music. President Andrew Oelhafen of the association will speak. Others will be asked to talk about early days in the city.

While it will be an old settlers' picnic, everybody is invited to attend and enjoy the occasion. The ladies of the association will serve hot coffee and the picnickers will furnish their own eatables, knives, forks, spoons and cups.

The members of the arrangement committee of the picnic are Mmes. O. K. Welty, Richard Dawson and Joseph A. Hall. They will also act as a dinner committee.

The entertainment committee is composed of Messrs. and Mmes. C. E. Macomber, chairmen; A. J. Olson, A. M. Pride and W. D. Lambert, Mrs. Mary E. Headstream, Miss Emogene Wentworth and Floyd A. Clark.

The officers of the association are: Andrew Oelhafen, president; Floyd A. Clark, secretary; C. E. Macomber, treasurer.

Ask for the La Porte line the next time you come to our store and let us show you how little it costs to dress in the height of fashion.—A. Wangard & Co.

A carload of Nails and Wire just received at Evenson's Hardware. Don't forget the place.

September 24, 1909

TWO HUNDRED AT PICNIC

Second Annual Meeting of Old Settlers' Association Largely Attended and Is Big Success.

Two hundred old settlers and others not among the first-comers gathered last Saturday at Bradley park for the second annual picnic of the Old Settlers' association. Although the weather was slightly cool, the day otherwise was ideal for the occasion. The crowd was jolly and the picnic proved a decided success.

The crowed gathered at 11 o'clock. At 12 o'clock, a picnic dinner was served. Following the dinner, the Very Rev. Fr. J. B. Schever, pastor of St. Mary's church, made a short address, at the close of which the assemblage gave three rousing cheers for Tomahawk. President Andrew Oelhafen of the association was master of ceremonies and also presided at the business session at which officers were elected and a decision reached to repeat the picnic next year. The new officers are:

President—Richard Dawson.
Secretary—Mrs. O. K. Welty.
Treasurer—C. E. Macomber.

The date selected for next year's picnic is Sept 1.

To add to the pleasure of the gathering, the launches of A. M. Pride and William Drever were sent to the park for the use of the picnickers.

October 1, 1909

More Work on Railroad Park

Mrs. A. E. McCrea, landscape architect for the Milwaukee road, spent Sunday in Tomahawk, a guest of friends. While here, she took steps for further improvement of the railway park, especially that part of it lying west of the tracks. The plan outlined includes the smoothing and cleaning of the big tract west of the tracks and the planting of 100 trees, and also shrubbery along the driveway to Bradley park. Mrs. McCrea expects to visit Tomahawk again next week to supervise the planting.

October 29, 1909

PLANTING AT RAILWAY PARK

Carload of Trees and Shrubbery Set Out in Tract West of Tracks. Mrs. McCrea Here.

A carload of shrubbery and trees were planted last Saturday in the railway park west of the tracks and at the entrance to Bradley park. Mrs. A. E. McCrae of Chicago, landscape architect for the Milwaukee road, was here to plan and supervise the planting. Some more work in the way of cleaning, leveling and seeding has been promised by the railway officials and when it is completed the park will be a credit not only to the railway, but to the city also. Tomahawk will show its appreciation by a guardianship to prevent damage of any kind in the park and by continuing civic improvement throughout the city. The M. T. & W. railway is also doing considerable work on its land adjoining the Milwaukee road tract so as to make the entrance to Bradley park as attractive as possible.

November 12, 1909

TO VOTE ON PARK QUESTION

Question of City Acquiring the Hog's Back to Be Submitted at the Coming Election.

Whether or not the city shall purchase Bradley park, known as the Hog's Back, will be submitted to the voters of Tomahawk at the coming election.

The Bradley company, owner of Tomahawk's already famous beauty spot, has offered to sell the park for $10,000 payable in annual installments to $10,000, the unpaid balance to bear 4 percent interest. The offer also defers the first payment until April 1, 1912.

At a special meeting of the common Council held Tuesday evening, by a unanimous vote, the city clerk was directed to prepare ballots for the purpose of voting on the proposition.

March 25, 1910

PARK PURCHASE AUTHORIZED

COMMON COUNCIL COMPLIES WITH REFERENDUM VOTE

Mayor and Clerk Instructed to Close Deal—Firemen Get Salary Raise from $600 to $900.

Purchase of Bradley park was authorized by the common council Tuesday evening at the adjourned April meeting. The action of the council was in compliance with the referendum vote on the park question had at the election April 5, when a vote of 447 to 35 in favor of the purchase was cast. Mayor M. C. Hyman and City Clerk James Kelly were authorized to close the deal with the Bradley company.

The proposition made to the common council by the Bradley company fixes the price of the park at $10,000 payable in five years, the outstanding balance to bear 4 per cent interest, and the first payment not to be made until 1912. It is hoped now to get this proposition changed to provide for payment in ten years.

April 15, 1910

PARK PURCHASE IS CLOSED

BEAUTY SPOT IS NOW PROPERTY OF THE CITY

Deal Calls for Payment of $10,000 in Ten Years—Park Commission Is Planned.

Bradley park is now the property of the city of Tomahawk.

The deal for the purchase of the tract of beautiful timber land was closed Wednesday, Mayor M. C. Hyman and City Clerk James Kelly representing the city and R. B. Tweedy the Bradley company.

The purchase price for this unsurpassed natural park is $10,000. The agreement calls for payment in ten years at $1,000 a year, the unpaid balance to bear interest at 4 per cent.

The first payment is deferred until April 1, 1911.

April 29, 1910

(Continued on next page)

"That the park may be properly cared for and preserved for the pleasure of future generations, a park commission will be created at once. Mayor M. C. Hyman has decided upon this step and will announce his appointments to the commission at the May council meeting next Tuesday. Immediate steps will be taken to prevent further washing out of the west bank of Prospect point by the Wisconsin river. The plan now is to drive piling at the edge of the bank and fill in behind with brush and other debris from the park. This step, it is believed, will stop the washing out of the soil of the bank and save the trees which are close to the water's edge.

"Parents should impress upon the minds of the children the fact that the park is theirs," said Mayor Hyman today, "and that they must do nothing to injure the trees and vines and other natural beauties of the place. The children should be taught to love the park, to realize that it is for use not only of this generation, but of the generations to come. Older folks, too, should never forget that the beauties of the park should be guarded and preserved at all times and do nothing themselves or allow others to injure or mar its beauty."

April 29, 1910

PARK COMMISSION NAMED

Mayor Appoints Board of Five Members to Look After City's Recent Purchase.

Members of a park commission were appointed by Mayor M. C. Hyman Tuesday evening at the June meeting of the common council. The appointments were confirmed by the council. The new park commissioners and the length of their terms are:

John W. Oelnafen, one year.
A. E. Sutliff, two years.
R. C. Thielman, three years.
W. T. Bradley, four years.
R. B. Tweedy, five years.

A fund of $250 was created for the use of the park commission by the council. Since the meeting, however, it has been learned that the money will not be available, the law prohibiting the appropriation of money in this way for park purposes. It will be necessary to include the sum needed for the park in the annual tax budget and the fund kept separately as are the other funds of the city. It may be necessary now to secure the money needed for the park this year by popular subscription.

June 10, 1910

FOURTH OF JULY PROGRAM

Parade

Parade forms at City Hall at 8 o'clock. Route of parade—From City Hall east on Somo avenue to Fourth street, south on Fourth street to Wisconsin avenue, west on Wisconsin avenue to Railroad street, north on Railroad street to Somo avenue, east on Somo avenue to Tomahawk avenue.

PRIZES: Mercantile and Industrial Floats—First prize, $20; second, $15; third, $10.

Most Comic Turnout—First prize, $10; second $5.

Best Decorated Automobile—First prize, $10; second, $5.

Ladies' Riding Contest—First prize, $8; second, $5; third, $2.

Judges: Floats—Drs. J. D. Cutter, G. R. Baker, L. M. Pearson. Automobiles—Drs. W. E. Wray, J. R. Dodd, W. I. Macfarlane. Ladies' Riding Contest—W. R. Piper, D. C. Jones, John W. Oelhafen.

Addresses—At Park

Patriotic Addresses by the Very Rev. Fr. J. B. Scheyer, Rev. L. C. Kirst, Rev. I. H. Lewis, Rev. F. W. Heberlein.

Counting of ballots for choice of name for Park and dedication of Park under new name.

Park Dedication Address—Hon. M. C. Hyman.

June 10, 1910

READY FOR BIG CELEBRATION

PLANS FOR FOURTH OF JULY ARE COMPLETED

Much Interest Aroused in Naming of Park—Out-of-Town Horses Coming for Speed Events.

Plans for the Fourth of July celebration are now completed. Great interest is being taken in the name which shall be given to the park now called the Hog's Back. A number of people think that it should be called the Hog's Back on account of the oddness of the name. Others think it should be called Bradley park in honor of the late W. H. Bradley.

There has been some misunderstanding among the women as to what was meant by the woman's riding contest in the parade. As explained to by one of the committee the woman who makes the best appearance, that is, the best rider, regardless of costume, will get the prize.

Decoration of the park was started Thursday morning. The owners of launches are busy decorating their crafts and buying new propellers for the boat race. The strings of electric lights on Wisconsin avenue were hung Thursday.

July 1, 1910

BRADLEY NEW NAME FOR PARK

MEMORY OF CITY'S FOUNDER HONORED IN POPULAR VOTE

Pleasure Ground Recently Purchased by City Loses Old Name of Hog's Back at Dedication.

"Bradley Park" was the name selected by popular vote July 4 for the Hog's Back, recently purchased by the city of Tomahawk for use as a public park. By a vote of 383 in a total of 569 ballots cast the memory of the late William H. Bradley, founder and prime mover in the early development of the city, was perpetuated by the choice of his name for the city's beautiful pleasure ground. The complete vote was:

Bradley Park	383
Hog's Back	97
Tomahawk Park	14
City Park	21
Tweedy Park	11
Prospect Point	9
Arbor Vitae Park	7
Riverside Park	5
Pine Park	4
Genevieve Park	2
National Park	2
Hog's Land	2
Highland Park	2
Hyman Park	1
Pleasant Hill	1
Pig's Back	1
Norway Park	1
Lamont Park	1

July 8, 1910

Park Board Issue Warning

It seems hardly improbable that it would become necessary for the park board to have to issue a warning to citizens and societies of this city that they must be more careful in the manner in which they leave refuse and paper lying on the ground in Bradley Park. Just recently it was necessary to employ a man for two days to remove the rubbish and refuse after a picnic and while the board was not so very averse to having the place cleaned yet they have only a small amount of money alloted them each year to spend on the parks and they must be very economical in the way in which it is distributed. It would be a very easy matter for those who make use of this beautiful spot to see that it is cleaned of refuse before leaving. Civic pride should be made use of and the park board will not have these things to contend with. The board has stated that unless this thing is stopped that severe measures will be enacted to curb this practise and have asked the editors of the Leader to call the attention of the citizens to this practise.

July 7, 1920

The park board has just had erected a new large number of new signs directing tourist traffic to the camping sites in Bradley Park and at the Fourth street bridge. The board have decided to allow the use of the "hogsback" for a camping site, it having been argued that the mosquitos were too thick for comfort at Mirror Lake. The new signs are being erected at all principal points of entrance to the city giving directions to the camping sites.

Both - June 29, 1922

PARK BOARD BUILDS NEW BATHING BEACH

The city park board is getting ready to eerct a new bath house on the Wisconsin river in Bradley Park which will be located at the foot path entrance to the park proper on the way to the "hogsback."

The river bottom has been dredged out leaving a nice sandy beach which has a gradual decline in deeper water. A log boom will be stretched across the mouth of the little bay which forms the beach in order to prevent drowning accidents. A bath house 14x28 feet in size will also be erected.

This new beach and bath house is for the use of women and children only, the men's and boy's bath house being farther west.

The site is a handy one and is located adjacent to the boat livery being operated by Carl Boll. Mr. Boll who helped in the preliminary work will also erect a water tabaggan for the use of the children.

CLUB MEMBERS LUNCH IN PARK

Annual Outdoor Meeting Brings Out Fair Crowd Tuesday Evening

The call of the outdoors was answered by sixty members of the Civic and Commercial Club at their annual outdoor meeting in Bradley Park on Tuesday evening and from the manner in which they disposed of the lunch that was served there must have been an added tang to their appetites.

The meeting was under the auspices of the Advertising and Tourist Committee who had arranged for the event somewhat out of the usual meeting date due to the fact that they had invited "Brownie" and the "Poor Cuss" of the Milwaukee Journal to be present. These gentlemen came across the state from Black River Falls to be present.

The supper consisted of beef steak, fried pike, potato salad, squaw dish, baked beans, buttered rolls, French pastry and coffee. The meal was cooked on the new camp site stove which has been donated to the city park board by C. H. Grundy. The park board has erected a new shelter near the band stand and will have the stove bricked in for permanent use. It is a regular army company cook stove and was proved to be an ideal article for camp site use. The club will keep a supply of wood on hand

Knicker Clad Stenographers of Big City Learn Art of Frying Bacon Over Campfires Under Pines of Bradley Park

(By Lawrence Eklund)

The tourist season is at its height at Bradley Park these days. Cars from every section of the country congregate under the great Norway pines which for many years past have aroused the admiration of visitors in Tomahawk.

Local merchants who are profiting by the tourist business this summer more than they usually do feel keenly the value of the park as an inducement to tourists. The park, originally costing the city $10,000, which was added to a $10,000 donation by the late Wm. Bradley, seems to be paying for itself.

A public park is especially valuable nowadays, when all of the lake frontages and pleasure places are being gobbled up by private enterprisers. Tomahawk may be thankful to her city fathers who had foresight enough to save a little bit of nature's heritage for society.

The local park took on the appearance of a war time army camp over the last week end, there were so many tents pitched. Some travelers who just dropped in casually to put up a tent for one night changed their minds and went no farther north, staying in Tomahawk for the whole length of their vacation. That is getting to be the custom with tourists who motor up this way.

It is a peaceful and arcadian scene out among the towering pines. Here the insurance salesman from New York pauses to talk about the price of wheat with a grain dealer from Iowa. Over a cheery campfire of resinous pine firewood, a thrifty Ohio housewife explains the most efficient method of frying bacon to a knicker clad stenographer from some Chicago business firm.

And above all can be heard the joyous laughter of city bred children who hitherto have played in man made parks only. Some of the older children, of the rather unsteady age of from 17 to about 22, have brought their musical instruments along, and so the long suffering pines must listen to the amorous wailings of youthful Romeos forcing their musical talent on coy maidens of chance acquaintance.

The park is a worthwhile and interesting place to visit right now. Even old residents of the city, who have seen the famous pleasure ground a hundred times before, will admit that the unusual influx of tourists has given the place an entirely different aspect.

July 9, 1925

Bradley Park is enjoying an unusually large run of tourists this summer and as usual everyone is overly enthusiastic about the beauties of the park. The Park Board are having a large number of tables with attached benches made for the convenience of the tourists and it is hoped that the townspeople—but perhaps more especially the Tomahawk boys will see that they are kept in good condition. A few years ago the Park Board had a few of these benches made and they were almost as quickly mutilated and it was done by home talent.

July 30, 1925

Mirror Lake in Bradley Park

Bradley Park Tourists Have Words of Appreciation for Fair Treatment

We have traveled through a dozen states and under all conditions and we have never had more courteous treatment than that which is accorded at the Bradley Park in Tomahawk. The nights are wonderful with nice central campfires nearly every night. These entertainments about the fires are purely non-professional and gratuitous. The folk carry up the brush and when the fire is on, stories begin. We have enjoyed the boys from the Legion post of Tomahawk. They have entertained us with popular songs several nights. Last Sunday evening they too could not resist the fire and came and mingled their songs with ours. This is something unusual and much appreciated by the scores of cheery folk camping at the park.

The Hull Quartet, on saxaphone, from Detroit have given us many pleasant treats. They not only play well but generously. Sunday night August 2, the Reverend Marvin M. Walters of Joy, Illinois, cooperated with the various musicians and after several musical numbers and hymns, the visiting Presbyterian pastor spoke to the crowd consisting of about a hundred folk on "The Vacations of Jesus" as a subject. The people seemed to like the religious services in the park Sunday evening.

Tomahawk is making another appeal to the tourists. The fairness of the business folk, their readiness to get and serve the campers with everything they want and at prices that are square makes a nice impression on all.

We find fishing good here and that all are willing to tell the tenderfoot where to go to get into the fishing game. We find that this little town slung in the cradle of lakes and rivers has taken the very generosity of nature for its slogan. Nothing is to be desired as far as visitors are concerned, from the services of the old gentleman, Mr. Haring, who keeps the park clean, to the mayor of the city who is more than willing to show one around. We appreciate the publicity of the paper in giving space to this word of appreciation.

Signed:
One of the Campers.

August 6, 1925

Horicon Tourists Have Words of Appreciation for Enjoyable Time Spent in Bradley Park Campsite

The following letter of appreciation was received the past week by John Bloomquist, who has been one of the boys responsible for the fine entertainments which have been accorded the tourists in Bradley Park this season. The letter was addressed "To John—the Star Singer at Bradley Park, Tomahawk, Wis."

Horicon, Wis.
August 8, 1925.

Camp Fire Friends:

After having camped at Bradley Park for a week, we can't help but let you know that pleasant memories turn our thoughts back to Bradley Park. The enjoyable time we had amidst the towering pines and the most congenial crowd we ever met, now seems but like a dream, but never will be forgotten.

Bayfield may boast about "the cream at the top" but when it comes to camping grounds, and efforts exerted by citizens of a community, Bradley Park and the citizens of Tomahawk cannot be too highly complimented on what they are doing for the tourists who come there. We now realize the reason why—the tented city in Bradley Park. May the people of Tomahawk prosper, and through their spirit of friendliness be blessed with greater rewards in the future.

This is the sincere wish of a group of friendly tourists.

Mr. and Mrs. Edw. Frei.
Mr. and Mrs. E. C. Ulrich.

August 13, 1925

The Legion band will give another concert at the Bradley Park on Friday evening of this week at which time it may be possible that some surprises will be in store for those who drive over and the tourists who are very appreciative of this music. The concert last Friday evening drew a large crowd and in addition to the band music, John Bloomquist sang several songs. The piano was furnished by Art Searl who had it put in shape and tuned so that it might be used for future concerts. Two young ladies among the tourists, also sang several songs and the crowd joined in several numbers.

August 13, 1925

Bradley Park Concert Draws Large Crowd

Between four and five hundred people crowded into Bradley Park to make up the largest gathering which we have seen in the park for several years, at the band concert and entertainment last Friday evening.

The program was mighty fine and enjoyed by not only the citizens present but also by the tourists who were stopping in the park and they voiced their appreciation at the close of the evening by giving a lusty "yell" for Tomahawk.

Besides the many fine numbers by the band, Mrs. Geo. Theiler and John Bloomquist both sang solos, while Mr. Bloomquist and Mrs. Theiler and Mr. Bloomquist and Roland Paul sang duets. In addition Mrs. Theiler sang a solo entitled "I've Lost My Soulmate" Mr. Paul having composed the music for the song and Mrs. Theiler having written the words. Another feature was some yodling by a gentleman visiting in the city which was greatly enjoyed.

The park was attractive with its new electric lights which are a great convenience for the tourists who still continue to patronize it in a liberal way.

August 20, 1925

Bradley Park Forms Traditions Say Campers

It is plain that there are some things about Bradley Park, Tomahawk, that are unique. The fact that many of the finest campers come and remain for several days and even weeks is a good omen. These form certain traditions. They make new comers welcome and help them get comfortably settled. Other camps are often full at night but empty in the day time, meaning that no traditions, no happy memories can form in the life of the camps.

The Sunday evening services and social hours have been great this season. The Rev. Marion M. Walters of Joy, Ill., preached twice at the camp fire on Sunday nights Aug. 2 and 9th, and the Rev. Dr. G. W. Sutton Ph. D. of the first Presbyterian church of Lincoln, Ill., spoke to the campers Sunday evening August 16th on the subject of "Rest."

The accomodating service at the boat house, the presence of Martin Kenney the crack fisherman, the visit of the Detroit Saxophone Quartet and the happy jokes of Bob Nichols of St. Louis and the quaint fish lies of Mr. Fridley of Chicago are high spots of the season.

No one can ever forget Mr. and Mrs. Culver and their genial reception of new comers and their interest in preparing camp fires.

So far this season twenty persons have come to the park from the little town of Joy, Illinois. Joy likes Tomahawk well and Joy has enjoyed many fine fish treats from their minister's hook. The pastor has spent two summer vacations here and has traveled to nearly all the good vacation spots in the country including the Great Northwest and Niagara Falls but he likes this little pine haven by the river best of all. These are the "Haunts of the swaying pines and chipping red squirrels." Long will we all remember thee.

Signed, A Happy Camper.

P. S. Who will ever forget the great kindness of the Tomahawk folks, the folks at the stores, the men at the banks and garages, the ministers of the churches and the genial folk at the Post Office and at the Leader.

August 20, 1925

More Evidence of Hospitality

Lincoln, Illinois,
September 8, 1925.

To the Editor of
The Tomahawk Press,
Tomahawk, Wisconsin.
My dear Sir:—

I wish to thank the Citizens of Tomahawk for a most pleasant and profitable outing spent at the beautiful Bradley Park. We have motored to many sections of our country and camped in many so called "Tourist Parks" but never before have we found one so beautiful as the Virgin Forest Norway Pine Bradley Park of Tomahawk. We arrived one evening expecting to go on to Rhinelander the next morning but we remained two weeks and never did go to Rhinelander. Your great number of fine lakes and splendid fishing spots satisfied us. The hospitality of your people, and especially that of Mr. H. A. VanGalder has never been surpassed by any city we have visited. We were carried away with the Park and lakes and your City. The Band concerts each week made us feel that you wanted us to stay with you. On top of all you did to make our vacation so pleasant, the tourists we met were of such high character that our fellowship at Bradley Park was indeed very happy. We made many fine friendships. We felt perfectly safe in leaving our tent and possessions at any time and everything was unmolested and yet the Park was not policed. The Sunday evening Church Service in which we participated undoubtedly helped greatly in giving this fine moral tone to the Park. We are greatly in your debt. We thank you again and again for our vacation spent at Bradley Park.

Cordially yours,
G. S. Sutton.

September 10, 1925

Prepare Ice Rink and Skii Slide for Winter Carnival

Convinced that Tomahawk offers just as much as our neighboring cities in the way of winter sports, a number of local business men have put their efforts toward a winter carnival which it is planned to hold within the next week or two.

It had first been planned to hold the event a week from Sunday, February 28th, but inasmuch as Minocqua is holding a similar event that day and have already advertised it extensively, those in charge here will probably put it off until the first Sunday in March.

A huge rink is being prepared on the Wisconsin river between Bradley Park and Raymond's mill, where a space 50 feet wide and 400 feet long has been cleared and is being flooded. Adjacent to the rink a skii slide is being erected under the supervision of S. B. Bugge and O. F. Duus.

Some of the leaders in this movement are M. M. Raymond, A. A. Searl, J. A. Fitzgerald and J. H. Floyd. They hope to have the rink ready for use by Saturday of this week when everyone is invited to use it, as use will improve it. Then too if there are those who would like to assist in the work they will be welcomed and should so advise any of the above gentlemen.

We shall be able to announce the dates and events of the carnival definitely next week.

February 18, 1926

2,500 People Watch First Winter Carnival

Day Ideal For Spectators But Bad For Ice; Entries From Eagle River, Rhinelander, and Wausau Vied For Prizes; Moving Pictures Taken During Day To Advertise City At Outdoor Exposition

BRADLEY PARK LIVERY SOLD TO JOHN PERMAN

The Bradley Park boat livery which last season was operated by C. C. Herrick of Union Grove last season has been sold to John Perman of this city. Mr. Perman advises us that he will be assisted in operating the livery this coming summer by his nephew Axel Permanson of Brooklyn, N. Y., who will come to Tomahawk about the first of May.

Mr. Perman will add a large number of boats to the fleet together with outboard motors, making at least twenty boats. The boat house and adjoining property will be fixed up in first class shape and the needs of fishermen will receive the very best attention he states.

April 1, 1926

BOAT HOUSES TO BE WRECKED

Park Board Orders Removal of Old Boat Houses in Bradley Park; New Officers Elected

Owners of old boat houses in Bradley Park will be ordered to remove the structures, it was decided at a meeting of the park board Thursday night.

Ed. MacDonald was elected president, and Dr. W. J. Macfarlane was elected vice president. Other board members are Mrs. J. R. Doht, Mrs. John Extrom and G. L. Grube.

"We have received many complaints concerning the dilapidated boat houses," Mr. MacDonald said Wednesday, "and we decided that if the buildings are not removed by their owners the board will have to do it."

The board also voted to comply with the Homecoming committee's request to clear Bradley Park of campers during the celebration which will be held July 3-4-5.

May 28, 1936

Boat House Bay

TOURISTS OFFER SUGGESTIONS

Dr. Rowe Baker and L. W. Osborne, who made the first official visit of the Kiwanis Club to Bradley Park last Friday evening to extend the "glad hand" to our campers, found it a most agreeable task.

That these daily visits of the Kiwanis Club members will be productive of good results is evidenced by the following set of resolutions which were received by Dr. Baker in the mail on Monday morning signed by some of the campers in the park:

TOURISTS IN SESSION AT BRADLEY PARK
July 9, 1927

WHEREAS, Dr. Baker and Mr. Osborne of the Tomahawk Kiwanis Club favored us with a friendly call last evening, the spirit of which was accepted and approved by all here gathered and acting on their requests for suggestions as to betterment of this camp as to improvements and facilities, a meeting was called this day and year above written, the following resolutions passed. Be it

RESOLVED, that a mop squad be appointed, the duty of which is to inspect at least once each week the ladies' toilets and to place such toilets in neat appearance by thorough cleaning—the gents can look out for themselves. Be it further

RESOLVED, that we here gathered appreciate the firewood furnished but to obtain necessary fuel with a small hand axe such as is carried by all tourists is a slow process like that unto a woodpecker, therefore be it

RESOLVED, that we here gathered suggest that a cross cut saw be furnished so that we may lighten the labor of furnishing the fuel for the good camp wife and in a way emulate Kaiser Bill with the saw. Be it further

RESOLVED, that we thank Tomahawk and all concerned for the privilege of using this ideal camp and further

RESOLVED, that these resolutions be accepted in the same spirit as adopted.

THE TOURIST COMMITTEE

July 14, 1927

BRADLEY PARK HARD TO BEAT
By
Marvin M. Walters (a camper)

Everything has a character all its own. Tomahawk is no exception in this regard. Nature has done a lot for Tomahawk. Its summer dress is the best among all the watering places of the country. The wide waters insure plenty of fish despite the swarm of fishermen ever plying about its superb shores. But clean aside of what the wild character of Tomahawk, is the human equasion. The people of this city are doing and have done everything that could be done to make a pleasant summering place. The management of Bradley Park is such as to guarantee finest use of the Park, and the very fairness of the local folk appeals to every comer. After spending four of my last five Augusts at Bradley Park I am prepared to say that its call comes louder every season. There is a feeling that one has as he swishes out and in among the many weed and pine islands that gets into one's heart and stays there through the years. That is what I call a vacation.

In all these years I have never heard one word of exaggeration regarding this part of Wisconsin. It does not seem to be in the hearts of the Tomahawk people nor the campers at Bradley Park to either commercialize or unduly parade the qualities of this outing quarter. This makes the very strongest appeal to the campers. We are, nearly everyone, just folks, and we like this plain treatment.

The business and home folks of Tomahawk are the most hospitable and thoughtful one can find in a week's travel. The prices at the stores are as fair and fine as are offered anywhere. The musical and other entertainment furnished gratis to the campers is very enjoyable. The nicety of arrangements in the Park makes practically every camper respect it and want to keep the rest rooms, the phone service and every other feature in good shape. There is bred into all of us a wholesome respect for the place.

So it has come about that we come again and again from year to year, each time to appreciate the place more, and able to spread good news of Tomahawk further and further.

I return to the matter of character again. This is the finest and most appealing thing in anything or person; and we all hope that Tomahawk will continue to have this inner something that mere words cannot display.

August 18, 1927

At least fifty outside riders will come to Tomahawk on Sunday, Jan. 22 to participate in the open tournament of the Tomahawk Ski Club who will hold their first meet of the season at their slide in Bradley park on that date. Clarence Birling, premier rider from the Noorie Ski club of Ironwood, Mich., will be present for demonstration rides and will act as one of the judges. A large number of the local club attended the meet at Minocqua last Sunday.

January 12, 1928

SKI JUMPERS TO GATHER HERE

Expert Rider From Ironwood, Mich., Will Make Exhibition Jumps and Act as One of Judges

Some fifty ski riders from all the neighboring cities will flock to Tomahawk next Sunday to participate in the first annual exclusive event of the Tomahawk Ski club, which will be held on their slide in Bradley Park beginning at 2 p. m.

Included in this galaxy of riders are some of the best known amateurs in this part of the state. The local club has divided the riders into classes and are offering prizes in each class. No professional riders will be allowed to compete for prizes.

As an attraction for the crowd which is expected, Clarence Berling of Ironwood, Mich., will give several exhibition rides and also act as one of the judges. Last Sunday at Minocqua Berling set a record jump of 97 feet but was unable to keep his balance on their tricky hill.

The local ski club are not making any charge for admission to this event but are offering tags to those who would like to help support the event for anything which they may wish to contribute. The club members report a generous response on the part of the public and this also predicts a large crowd at the event.

Speed Calls for Caution

This is an age of speed. Every make of automobile now going on the market for 1928 is faster than before. It is faster for the ordinary, everyday use, not just for test purposes. The automobile manufacturers have met the demand for swifter machines. But unless traffic regulations are strictly observed, 1928 is likely to see an unprecedented number of lives sacrificed on the altar to the god of speed.

The situation calls for a general tightening up on the part of those responsible for the enforcement of the speed laws. Pedestrian and motorist alike must be forced to obey the law or be punished. It is better that they suffer mildly than that they die.

If both motorists and pedestrians obey the rules, many lives will be saved and nobody will be really inconvenienced. And if everybody will obey the regulations, traffic will move faster, too. Don't take a chance, for you may make it your last one.

January 19, 1928

BIG CROWD OUT FOR SKI EVENT

Thirty-Five Riders From Neighboring Cities Participated in First Annual Open Event of Local Ski Club

Despite the fact that the weather was pretty snappy last Sunday, a fairly large crowd turned out for the first annual open invitation meet of the Tomahawk Ski Club, but they didn't stay long and by the close of the last event, the crowd had dwindled to almost the riders themselves.

Thirty-five riders from neighboring cities were on hand for the meet and are loud in their praise on the manner in which the meet was conducted. Outside riders walked away with all the prizes offered.

Clarence Berling, star rider of the Norrie Athletic club of Ironwood, Mich., acted as head judge of the events and also made several exhibition rides. His jumps averaged between 90 and 100 feet and he showed perfect form in the takeoff and landing, acting almost like a big bird as he swooped down off the slide.

Tomahawk entries included Francis Stutz, Chas. Baumgartner, Ralph Baumgartner, Earl Cronkrite, Wilfred LaVigne, E. R. Lavers, Joe Rosek, John Miller, Wilfred Wandeen, Frances Dewing and Oscar Copes.

January 26, 1928

Last Ski Meet of Winter Comes Next Sunday

The Tomahawk Ski Club will hold their last open meet of the season at the Bradley Park slide next Sunday afternoon, March 4, beginning at 2 o'clock.

The local club have put up several prizes for the event dividing the riders into two classes. Three prizes are being offered in each class and also a prize for longest standing jump in each class. The hill will be open to outside riders for practicing until noon Sunday.

All of the best riders who have taken part in meets in this vicinity during the past winter have been invited to attend and most of these have already accepted. These include Oscar Neimark and Harold Jensen of Rhinelander, Palmer Peterson of Woodruff, Victor Anderson and Joe Freebourn of Antigo and Bud Tapley of Minocqua.

The coming meet will be financed through the sale of tags as in the first meet here this winter. An entrance fee of 50 cents for senior riders and 25 cents for junior riders is being made. Entries should be mailed or handed to E. B. Lavers, secretary of the Tomahawk Ski club.

March 1, 1928

As has been the custom for the past several years, the city will observe Independence Day on July 4th with a celebration under the auspices of the local post of the American Legion. As now planned, the celebration will not be a pretentious affair but more in the nature of a big picnic and will be held in Bradley park. The program will be arranged especially for the benefit of the children. A committee will be appointed at once by W. G. Bauman, commander of the post to rarange the program and details.

June 7, 1928

PREPARING FOR 4TH PROGRAM

Legion Plans For Monster Picnic in Bradley Park During Afternoon; Fireworks Will Feature Evening Program With Dance

We are sorry that we are unable to give a complete program of the celebration here next week Wednesday, when the local American Legion post will sponsor a celebration in Bradley Park in the form of an old fashioned picnic.

Committees are now at work on the program for the afternoon and announcement will be made later. It is expected that there will be the usual races and contests for the children, for the program is being arranged primarily for the kiddies.

In the evening there will be an unusual display of fireworks. This will be under the supervision of Walter Caron. A representative of the company who will furnish the fireworks was in the city all day Monday putting together the large set pieces which will be a feature of the display.

A big dance at the Eagles club with Chippey Roberges' orchestra will complete the day's festivities.

June 28, 1928

PARK PROJECT IS PROGRESSING

Construction of New Kitchen Is In Progress at City's Famed Bradley Park; Plan Other Improvements

Bradley park is undergoing a rapid and radical physical transformation these days.

Its usual, sequestered winter existence has been disturbed as a crew of WPA workmen has been rushing to completion the construction of a new park kitchen to accommodate the summer colony of tourists who annually populate the scenic spot. It is located just south of the band stand.

Of split stone construction, the kitchen, when finished, will be 26 feet wide, 47 feet long, and about 16 feet high. It will have a concrete floor and a shangled roof and will include two fire places, one on either end of the structure. One of the fireplaces will be a heating unit, the other a cooking fireplace, replete with flues, grates, and ventilating construction. Both will be made of attractive flagstone work.

February 5, 1942

Kettle Hoist

Rafters and trusses in the kitchen will be made of rustic, cut logs, and a small "derrick" will be installed above the heating fireplace so that a large "stew kettle" can be hoisted out over the fire.

Another building, a comfort station, will also be started soon in the park, according to the local WPA headquarters. This building, which will be 26x 22 feet, will be situated west of the kitchen and will be partitioned off to house toilet facilities for both men and women. Like the kitchen, the bath house will also be of split stone construction and will be roofed with white cedar shingles.

Present plans are for the installation of a furnace and a fuel room in the basement of the bathhouse, but it was pointed out that part of the basement space could be set aside for winter sports purposes if necessary. It is also planned to drill a well in the bathhouse basement.

Make Footbridges

In connection with the bathhouse, septic tanks will be buried in the immediate area, according to WPA officials. They reported that several smaller projects have already been completed, including the construction of a log footbridge across the slough between Bradley park and Mirror lake and considerable roadwork. Two other footbridges are to be built in the near future, it was said.

Other units in the project to be started when possible are: 20 acres of timber stand improvement; construction of one mile of foot and ski trails and 50 stone fireplaces throughout Bradley park, construction of 50 rustic signs, construction of double tennis court on city-owned property in downtown area, construction of 50 rustic log benches, grading of one mile of park roads, placing of 72 guard posts, and other miscellaneous work, including riprapping of roadways bordering banks of small water bodies.

About 20 men are constantly employed on the project.

February 5, 1942

Bugged

The majestic pines of Bradley park, some over 200 years old, have been infected for the past two summers by an invasion of pine bark beetles, which burrow between bark and wood, opening the way for harmful fungi.

July 7, 1977: Pine Bark Beetle infestation

July 7, 1977

> **NO CAMPING**
>
> AN INFESTATION OF PINE BARK BEETLES IN THIS AREA HAS PLACED THESE 200 YEAR OLD TREES IN SERIOUS DANGER IN ORDER TO AVOID PUTTING THE TREES UNDER THE ADDITIONAL STRAINS PRODUCED BY SOIL COMPACTION AND ROOT INJURY THE TOMAHAWK CITY PARK BOARD HAS ORDERED THAT NO CAMPING BE ALLOWED IN BRADLEY PARK DURING 1977

Beetles Plague Bradley Pines

Once again the pine bark beetle has infected Bradley park, causing the City Park Board to close the park to campers for 1977.

There are over 2,000 species of bark beetle, and hundreds of them have been known to attack pines. Since blazes or cuts on a tree attract the beetle, traffic and vandalism caused by campers could worsen the problem at the park.

The pine beetle is about a quarter inch long and burrows under the bark, but must gnaw holes through the bark to release excrement. It has two common natural predators in the area, the woodpecker and a cannibal called the ant beetle.

One particularly damaging aspect of the bark beetle is that it often opens the way for various diseases and fungi to infect the tree, which could severely damage a tree or cause an epidemic in the forest.

The 200-year old pines in Bradley park are not in critical danger because of the beetle, however the problem could worsen without careful management and the cooperation of park visitors.

Bradley Park Camping Is Council Topic

Closing Bradley park to overnight camping will come before the Tomahawk city council tonight (Thursday) at its April session.

The meeting -- at 8 p.m. in the city hall -- was postponed from Tuesday because of the spring election.

No vote on the park proposal is scheduled Thursday, Clerk Bud Hupfer indicated.

The park board closed the park to overnight campers the past two summers because of possible root damage to trees that were susceptible to the pine bark beetle because of dry weather.

April 6, 1978

BOARD, COUNCIL AGREE

No Camping in Park

For the third consecutive year, summer visitors to Tomahawk won't be allowed to camp overnight in Bradley park, the city park board decided last week.

City council members tacitly endorsed extending the camping ban during a regular meeting April 6.

The park board voted 5-0 April 18 to extend indefinitely the two-year ban on overnight camping in the city park. But the park board will issue special permits for local scout camping.

Bradley park was closed to overnight camping two years ago by the park board because camping activities aggravated damage to trees caused by an infestation of pine bark beetles and drought. Many of the trees in the park are well over 200 years old.

The park was originally owned and established by William Bradley, the lumber baron who was one of the principal planners of the city in 1887. Bradley prohibited logging in the park, which sits on a peninsula extending into the Wisconsin river.

Non-residents were charged $3.50 per night to camp there. There was no charge for city residents. Vandals caused considerable damage to park buildings before and after the park was closed to campers. The park's custodian retired last year.

Second Ward Ald. Harold Burton maintained three weeks ago during a council meeting that the park should be re-opened to tourist camping, stating that the park should be available for use by tourists and residents alike.

Former Second Ward Ald. Howard Hetzel, who has lived near the park for more than 40 years, refuted claims of vandalism damage.

But Third Ward Ald. Merlin Hanke and Fourth Ward Ald. Albert Daigle maintained that camping in the park should be restricted to city residents and said city residents should be the principal beneficiaries of the park.

"There are enough commercial campgrounds (in this area) to serve tourist campers," Daigle commented.

Third Ward. Ald. Darwin Sweeney urged the council to follow the recommendations of the park board but supported a suggestion to allow local Boy and Girl Scouts to camp in the park with a special permit.

The park board last week also discussed placing additional restrictions on use of motorcycles and automobiles in the park. City ordinance prohibits operating a motor vehicle off park roads. The park board will post more signs in the park to remind motorists to stay on designated roads.

The park board will plant about 80 trees along city boulevards in a continuing program to replace nearly 2,000 diseased elm trees that have been removed. The park board will replace only trees that were on city property. Private property owners must replace diseased trees that were removed by city crews if they want new trees. About 200 city elm trees were cut down this year.

The city's tree-planting program was delayed last year because of drought. Replacement trees will include several varieties of ash, hard and soft maple, locust, linden, flowering crab and oak. The trees will be about eight feet tall and two inches in diameter. They were chosen for their hardiness and variety of colors and shapes.

The council allocated $2,500 for tree replacement in 1978, an increase of about $1,000 over 1977.

City residents who want tree stumps removed from their private property should contact private stump removal companies instead of the city.

April 27, 1978

NOTICE!

BRADLEY PARK IS CLOSED TO ALL VEHICLES DAILY FROM 7 P.M. TO 7:00 A.M. UNTIL FURTHER NOTICE, DUE TO CONSTANT AND EXCESSIVE VANDALISM.

THE BRADLEY PARK SHELTER HOUSE WILL BE OPENED TO VEHICLES AFTER 7 P.M. UNDER PERMITS FOR GATHERING ISSUED BY THE CITY CLERK.

BY ORDER OF
MAYOR WILLIS GESSLER
City of Tomahawk

July 13, 1978

Imposed park hours due to increased vandalism

Owens-Illinois Picnic

The biggest crowd ever was on hand Monday for the annual Labor Day picnic at Bradley park. Attending were O-I, Northern Woodlands and M T & W railroad employees, Draxo company employees, who are constructing an expansion project at the mill, and the project's engineers.
—Leader Staff

September 7, 1978

For years, O-I held an annual Labor Day picnic for employees in the park.

'Illegal Structures' —Leader Staff

The state Division of Natural Resources Hearings has given these boat houses 180 days to live — at least at their present site. The buildings are on Lake Mohawksin near the entrance to Bradley park. The Department of Natural Resources said they were illegal structures and a hearing examiner agreed. The boat house at left is owned by Theodore Marquardt, Scott Stevenson and Mike Kolat, all of Tomahawk. The one at right is owned by Sigward Watten, Rhinelander, and the estate of Fred Watten.

March 22, 1979

Situated in the park is a log cabin, built in the 1930's by Carl Nystrom, then city police officer and park ranger. Camping in the park was permitted at that time, and the log cabin served as a registration office for campers. It went unused for many years and fell into disrepair.

When the city was considering its demolition, the Tomahawk Area Historical Society stepped in and restored it in 2003 along with the Tomahawk City Parks Department. Electricity was brought into the building; however, the cabin has not been used since. The cabin was aptly named after Nystrom, the builder and the city's only law enforcement officer to die in the line of duty.

Patrolman Carl Nystrom was shot and killed while attempting to serve a warrant on a known felon on a train in Tomahawk, Wisconsin on Saturday, June 9, 1945. He is survived by a wife and child.

The 30-year-old suspect was apprehended, convicted of murder, and sentenced to life. He died in prison on September 11, 1970.

2014

2014

2014

2014

2018

2018

Cross Country Skier - Bradley Park 1978

About the Author

Robin L. Comeau, grew up on a farm just south of Tomahawk in the township of Skanawan. Residing in Buffalo, NY since 1987, she considers herself a lifelong student of history and folklore of the Tomahawk area. A graduate of the State University at Buffalo with a B.A. in History and Masters in Library Science, authored "Boom Town: Early History of Tomahawk, Wisconsin 1886-1924", "Merrill – Images of America" Arcadia series, co-author of "The Mill-Pond: A Lifetime of Tripoli Memories with Larry R. Peil", and compiled and edited "Spirit Falls: This Place I Call Home", by Dona Jahn. Comeau, a volunteer for the Tomahawk Area Historical Society acts as webmaster for the society's website. She hopes to use this work as a step toward placing Bradley Park on the Wisconsin State Historic Register.

Every place has a story; everyone has a legacy.

Made in the USA
Monee, IL
06 November 2021